Facts About the Grizzly Bear

By Lisa Strattin

© 2019 Lisa Strattin

D1714864

Facts for Kids Picture Books by Lisa Strattin

Little Blue Penguin, Vol 92

Chipmunk, Vol 5

Frilled Lizard, Vol 39

Blue and Gold Macaw, Vol 13

Poison Dart Frogs, Vol 50

Blue Tarantula, Vol 115

African Elephants, Vol 8

Amur Leopard, Vol 89

Sabre Tooth Tiger, Vol 167

Baboon, Vol 174

Sign Up for New Release Emails Here

http://LisaStrattin.com/subscribe-here

Monthly Surprise Box

http://KidCraftsByLisa.com

Contents

INTRODUCTION

The Grizzly Bear is a sub-species of the Brown Bear, also known as the Silvertip Bear. They live in the uplands of western North America, and each female has a litter of cubs roughly every other year.

CHARACTERISTICS

Grizzly bears can often be seen gathering together around streams during the salmon season to get the best catch. Normally, the Grizzly is generally a solitary mammal.

APPEARANCE

Grizzly Bear coat colors are different from region to region. They can be dark brown to reddish brown, they can also be black or very light beige. These bears have long white-tipped hairs along their shoulders and back, which gives the bear a "grizzled" appearance.

REPRODUCTION

Females that have cubs will often be extremely cautious of other animals. The mother will often keep her cubs in quieter areas until the cubs are older and big enough to defend themselves. At this time, the cubs will stray away from their mother in order to begin a their own life of roaming around. Mothers however, are very protective of their young and will usually attack any animal that she believes is a danger to her young family.

LIFE SPAN

Grizzly Bears live for 15 to 25 years.

SIZE

Male Grizzly Bears can grow to a height of more than 9 feet tall when standing on their hind legs, with females being smaller. The bears have a humped look at the top of their back, which is the buildup of the huge muscle that gives the bears the strength they need.

HABITAT

Grizzly Bears live in woodlands, forests, alpine meadows, and prairies. In many regions they prefer to live in areas along rivers and streams.

DIET

Although it is generally believed that the Grizzly Bear is a meat-eater, they, as with most other bear species, are omnivores. This means they eat both plants and animals.

The Grizzly Bear is most well-known for its love of salmon and can often be seen in large groups around the waterways where the salmon spawn. They are very territorial, but appear to stay out of each other's way when catching salmon, because there is always plenty of fish to go around during the spawning season.

ENEMIES

The Grizzly Bear has a bad reputation with humans and animals alike, as they are known to be aggressive and territorial. Because of the bear's size, there are no known North American animals that would naturally prey on them, making them an extremely dominant predator.

It is estimated that less than 10% of grizzly bears make it into full adulthood. While the grizzly bear has no natural predators, the bears have been hunted by humans almost to extinction.

SUITABILITY AS PETS

Grizzly Bears are not suitable as pets. You can see them at many zoos around the country. If you have a local zoo, there is probably a bear habitat where you can see some bears, perhaps even the mighty Grizzly!

COLOR ME

COLOR ME

COLOR ME

COLOR ME

COLOR ME

COLOR ME

Please leave me a review here:

http://lisastrattin.com/Review-Vol-285

For more Kindle Downloads Visit Lisa Strattin Author Page on Amazon Author Central

http://amazon.com/author/lisastrattin

To see upcoming titles, visit my website at LisaStrattin.com– all books available on kindle!

http://lisastrattin.com

PLUSH GRIZZLY BEAR TOY

You can get one by copying and pasting this link into your browser:

http://lisastrattin.com/PlushGrizzlyBear

MONTHLY SURPRISE BOX

Get yours by copying and pasting this link into your browser

http://KidCraftsByLisa.com

Made in the USA
Monee, IL
03 May 2020